A Note to Parents

DK READERS is a compelling program for beginning readers, designed in conjunction with leading literacy experts, including Dr. Linda Gambrell, Distinguished Professor of Education at Clemson University. Dr. Gambrell has served as President of the National Reading Conference, the College Reading Association, and the International Reading Association.

Beautiful illustrations and superb full-color photographs combine with engaging, easy-to-read stories to offer a fresh approach to each subject in the series. Each DK READER is guaranteed to capture a child's interest while developing his or her reading skills, general knowledge, and love of reading.

The five levels of DK READERS are aimed at different reading abilities, enabling you to choose the books that are exactly right for your child:

Pre-level 1: Learning to read
Level 1: Beginning to read
Level 2: Beginning to read alone
Level 3: Reading alone
Level 4: Proficient readers

The "normal" age at which a child begins to read can be anywhere from three to eight years old. Adult participation through the lower levels is very helpful for providing encouragement, discussing storylines, and sounding out unfamiliar words.

No matter which level you select, you can be sure that you are helping your child learn to read, then read to learn!

LONDON, NEW YORK, MUNICH,
MELBOURNE, AND DELHI

DK LONDON
Series Editor Deborah Lock
US Senior Editor Shannon Beatty
Illustrator Jason Bays
Production Editor Francesca Wardell

Reading Consultant
Linda B. Gambrell, Ph.D.

DK DELHI
Editor Nandini Gupta
Art Editors Shruti Soharia Singh, Jyotsna
DTP Designer Anita Yadav
Picture Researcher Aditya Katyal
Dy. Managing Editor Soma B. Chowdhury

First American Edition, 2014
Published in the United States by DK Publishing
345 Hudson Street, New York, New York 10014

14 15 16 17 10 9 8 7 6 5 4 3 2 1
001—195863—February/2014

Published in Great Britain by Dorling Kindersley Limited.

A catalog record for this book is available from the Library of Congress.

ISBN: 978-1-4654-1720-6 (Paperback)
ISBN: 978-1-4654-1603-2 (Hardcover)

DK books are available at special discounts when purchased in bulk for sales promotions, premiums, fund-raising, or educational use.
For details, contact:
DK Publishing Special Markets
345 Hudson Street, New York, New York 10014
SpecialSales@dk.com

Printed and bound in China by
South China Printing Company.

The publisher would like to thank the following for their kind permission to reproduce their photographs:
a=above, b=below/bottom, c=center, l=left, r=right, t=top
6 **Dreamstime.com** Marcio Silva (tl). 8 **Dorling Kindersley**: Dave King/Graham High at Centaur Stidios - modelmaker (bl). 9 **Dorling Kindersley**: Andrew Kerr (tr). 11 **Dorling Kindersley**: Jon Hughes/Bedrock Studios (br). 12 **Dorling Kindersley**: John Hughes (br). 14 **Dorling Kindersley**: Colin Keates/Natural History Museum, London (tr). 19 **Dorling Kindersley**: Andy Crawford (br). 23 **Dorling Kindersley**: Colin Keates/ Natural History Museum, London (br). 25 **Dorling Kindersley**: Jon Hughes (cr). 25 **Dorling Kindersley**: Andrew Kerr (br). 30 **Dorling Kindersley**: Colin Keates/ Natural History Museum, London (tl); **Dorling Kindersley**: Andrew Kerr (cl); Jon Huhes (clb); Colin Keates/Natural History Museum, London (bl); **Dreamstime.com** Marcio Silva (cla).
All other images © Dorling Kindersley Limited
For further information see: www.dkimages.com

Discover more at

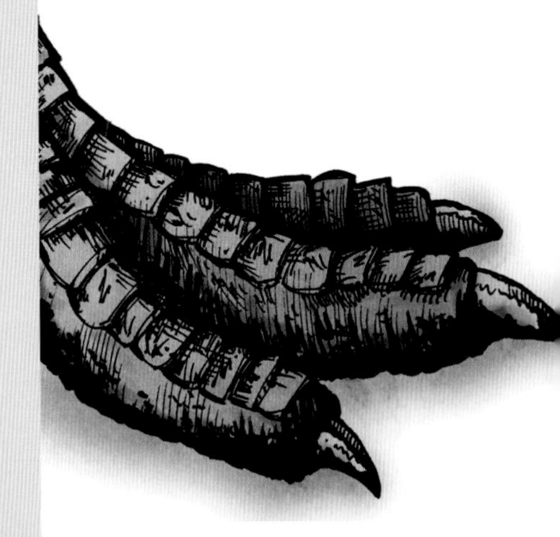

Deadly Dinosaurs

Written by Niki Foreman

It was nighttime
at the Dinosaur Museum.
No one was around.

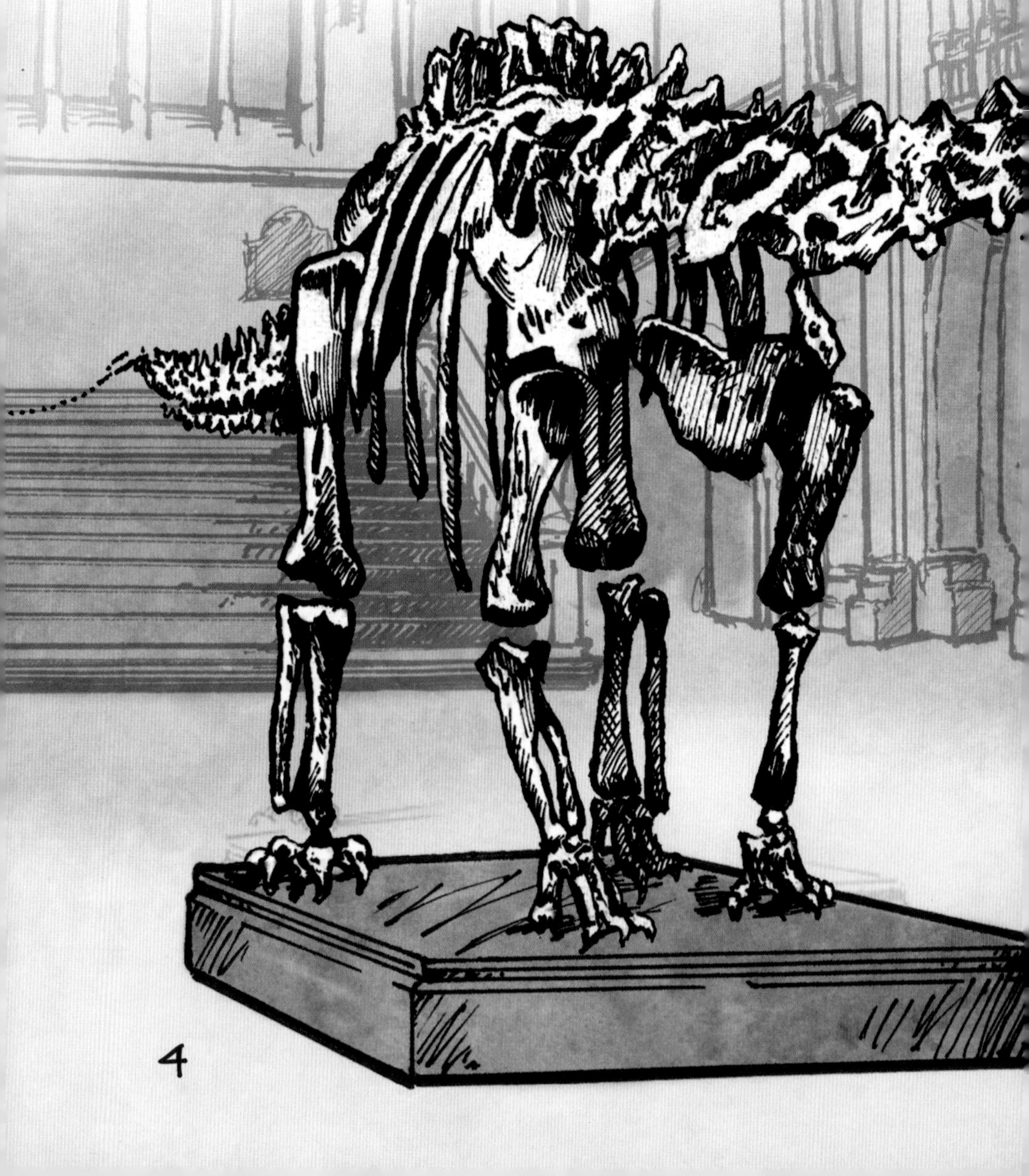

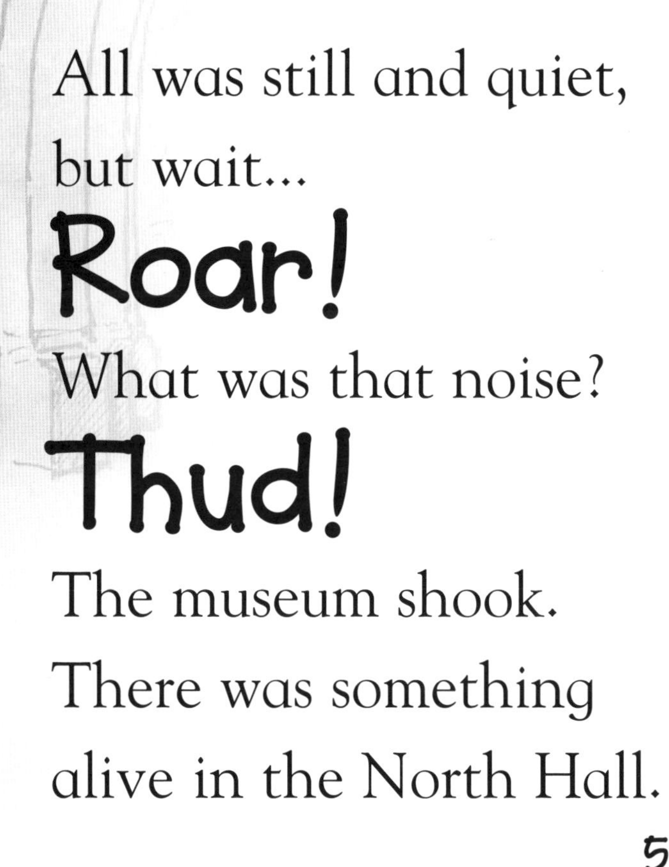

All was still and quiet,
but wait...

Roar!

What was that noise?

Thud!

The museum shook.
There was something
alive in the North Hall.

fossil

The North Hall was
full of fossils.
The fossils were the bones of
dead dinosaurs.
But there was something else
there, too—
something alive
and hungry!

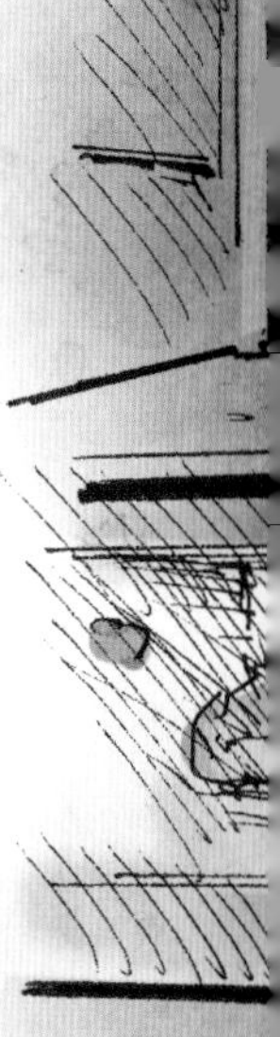

It stood up tall on two legs.
It had a long, stiff tail.

Swish!

Its teeth were sharp
like spikes.
It looked big and scary.
It was Rexy,
the *Tyrannosaurus Rex*.

Here is how to say
Tyrannosaurus Rex:
tie-RAN-oh-SOR-us-recks

ROAR!

The dinosaur models were alive!

model

Rexy was the best hunter around.
His sight was sharp.
He was fast and strong.
His huge jaws could bite into animals.

Crunch!

He could eat an *Edmontosaurus* alive, bones and all!

Here is how to say *Edmontosaurus*:
ed-MON-toh-SOR-us

Rexy was hungry.
He was drooling.

Slop!

His drool dripped on
something small at his feet.
It was Sid, the *Sinornithosaurus*.

Here is how to say
Sinornithosaurus:
SIE-nor-ni-thoh-SOR-us

Sid was hungry, too.

RASSSSP!

tooth

Sid shook the drool off
his feathers.
His long, sharp teeth gleamed
in his beak.
Something moved.
Sid pounced.
He sunk his teeth into its flesh.

ROAR!

It was Rexy's foot!

Sid had a killer bite.
His teeth were loaded
with poison, but
they were too small
to harm Rexy.
Sid gulped.
"Sorry, Rexy!"

Slop!

Another drip of drool
landed on him.

Deano, the *Deinonychus*,
pranced across the hall.

Thump!
Thump!

His long tail swept
from side to side.

Swish!

His two hooked claws tapped
on the floor.

Tap! Tap!

Here is how to say
Deinonychus:
die-NON-ee-kus

"You are such a featherbrain,
Sid!" drawled Deano.
"Biting old Rexy like that.
Tut tut.

Stick to your diet
of little dinosaurs.
Leave the big dinosaurs
to me!”

"You should see me hunt
with my friends.
We can kill a dinosaur
three times our size!
They call us the 'terrible claws'.
One slash from
these sharp claws
and dinner is ready."

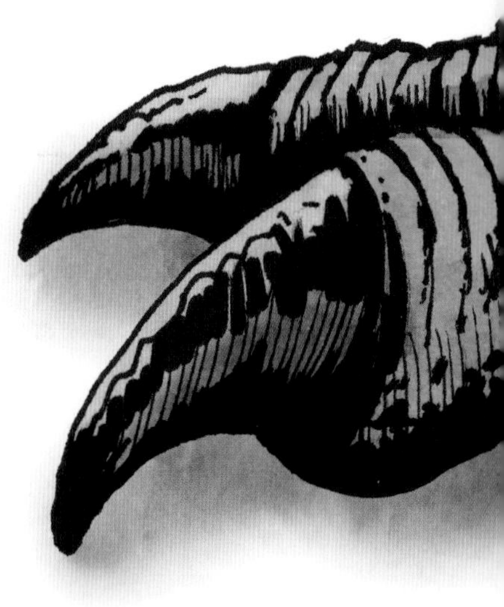

Slash!

claw

"Did someone say 'dinner'?"
hissed Sonia, the *Spinosaurus*.

Her toothy snout sniffed for fish.
The sail on her back stood
tall and grand.
She was the biggest dinosaur.

"I am the most deadly
dinosaur," hissed Sonia.
"Oh no, you are not!" roared
Rexy, Sid, and Deano.

"I am faster than Rexy,"
hissed Sonia.
"I have a more powerful bite
than Sid.
I do not need help to kill
like Deano.
I am the most deadly."

"Oh no, you are not.
I am!" hissed Sonia.
"Sh!" rasped Sid,
"I hear footsteps."
"It is the museum guard,"
said Deano.
"Back to your places,"
roared Rexy.

FREEZE!

All was still and quiet
in the North Hall.

Glossary

Claw
sharp curved nail
on a hand or foot

Fossil
remains of animals
and plants that lived
a long time ago

Model
copy of an object
or an animal

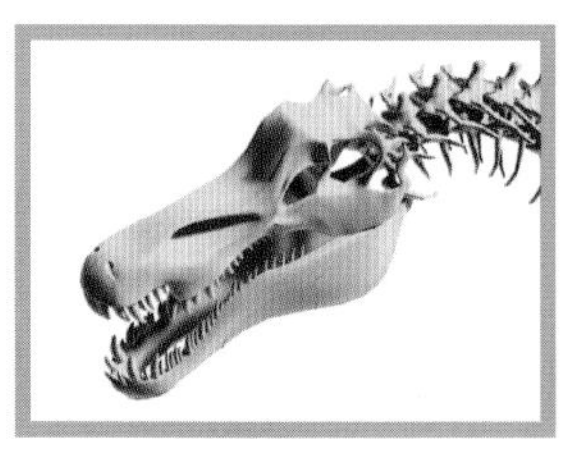

Snout
nose and mouth of an
animal that sticks out

Tooth
mouth part used for
chewing, cutting, or
tearing food

Index

DK READERS help children learn to read, then read to learn. If you enjoyed this DK READER, then look out for these other titles ideal for your child.

Level 1 Pirate Attack!
Come and join Captain Blackbeard and his pirate crew for an action-packed adventure on the high seas.

Level 1 LEGO® Legends of Chima™: Tribes of Chima
Enter the mysterious land of Chima™ and discover the amazing animal tribes who live there. Meet the Ravens, the Gorillas, the Eagles, the Crocodiles, the Lions, and the Wolves. But beware! Are they friends or foes?

Level 2 The Great Panda Tale
The zoo is getting ready to welcome a new panda baby. Join the excitement as Louise tells of her most amazing summer as a member of the zoo crew. What will the newborn panda look like?